DATES IN THE STATES

A COUPLE TRAVELING THE UNITED
STATES ON A BUDGET

Mystery Date
Webster, NY

By Dates in the States

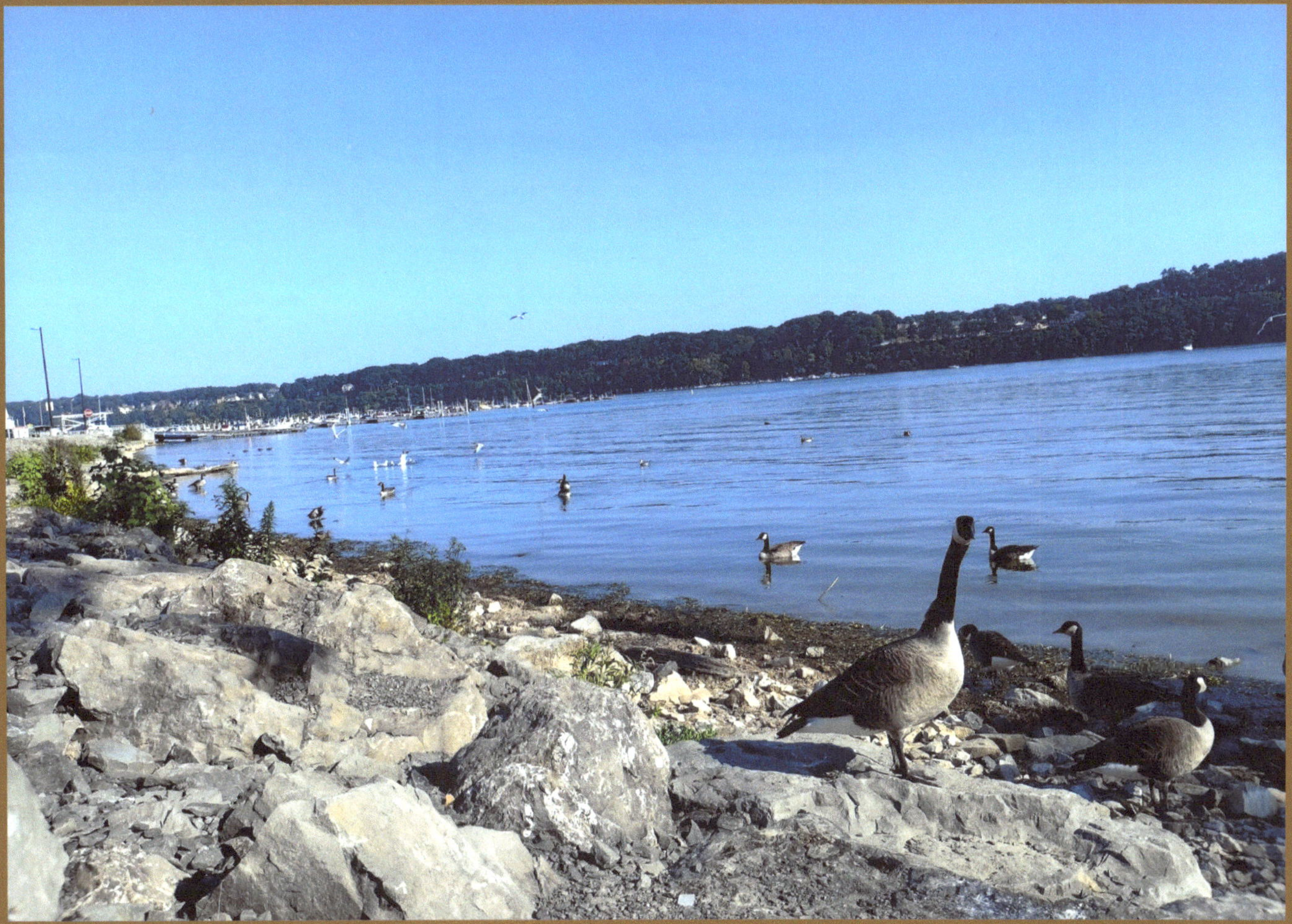

"Our passion is travel, and we want to share our adventures to inspire others to explore the world with their loved ones. Dare to live beyond the box."

Dates in the States

Introduction

Hey there! We're Crystal and Shane, the duo behind Dates in the States, where we share our love for discovering unique adventures, unforgettable moments, and hidden gems across the U.S. Whether you're searching for a fun date idea, a new place to explore, or just a little inspiration, we've got you covered!

Our Mystery Date Books are designed to help couples (and adventurous friends!) shake up their routine and experience the best local spots in a fun, intentional way. Inside, you'll find a curated collection of date ideas—each one meant to be completed over the course of a single day in a specific neighborhood. All of which are a surprise until you flip the page!

It's like a little challenge to break out of your comfort zone, support local, and make memories that stick. We hope this book helps you laugh more, explore more, and connect more—with each other and with your city. Let the mystery begin!

Here's What To Expect:

Get ready for a charming day in Webster, NY—a mix of cozy cafés, small-town charm, and delicious food. This date will guide you through the town's best spots, from unique shops to local history.

Start at a cozy café with your favorite brew, then stroll to a charming bookstore to browse for your next read. Next, step into Webster's past with a visit to a local museum. Wander Main Street to explore boutiques, quirky shops, and hidden gems.

Wrap up your adventure with a flavorful meal at a popular Mexican restaurant, offering bold flavors and a lively atmosphere.

Whether you're on a date or enjoying a solo adventure, this Mystery Date offers the perfect mix of small-town vibes, cultural experiences, and a delicious ending to your day.

Start

Village Bakery & Cafe

44 East Main St,
Webster, NY 14580

Begin your adventure at The Village Bakery with a warm latte, coffee, or tea, paired with a freshly baked treat. Stop by around lunchtime for a light snack before starting your day ahead.

A beloved local chain throughout Rochester, The Village Bakery is known for its inviting atmosphere and delicious menu. (The chocolate croissant is a must-try!) Whether you're craving a hearty breakfast sandwich, a flaky, buttery pastry, or a refreshing smoothie, there's something for everyone.

Once you have your drink in hand, take a short stroll over to Yesterday's Muse Books, a charming bookstore filled with rare, used, and new books waiting to be discovered.

Second Stop

Yesterday's Muse Books

32 West Main St,
Webster, NY 14580

Your next stop is Yesterday's Muse Books. Feel free to take your Village Bakery beverage inside with you while you hunt for your next read—just be mindful! Step into this haven for book lovers, filled with rare, used, and new books. Your task? Pick out a book that reminds you of your date—whether it's an adventure novel, a classic romance, or a quirky title that makes you laugh together.

Take a selfie with the book and purchase it if you'd like! We're all about supporting small businesses. Yesterday's Muse Books also sells our Mystery Date Books! See if you can find them, snap a photo, and share it on social media.
Be sure to tag us @datesinthestates and @yesterdaysmuse

Third Stop

The Webster Museum

18 Lapham Park
Webster, NY 14580

Step into The Webster Museum, where the history of Webster, NY comes to life through engaging exhibits. The museum offers a glimpse into Webster's past, from its agricultural roots to its early industrial development and growth as a modern-day community.

Inside, you'll find a collection assembled over many years—treasured items from Webster's early settlers, vintage photographs, costumes, and memorabilia from schools, community groups, and churches that reflect the town's rich heritage. Period rooms, a recreated drugstore, a lawyer's office, and a general store provide an immersive look at everyday life in different eras.

Just be sure to check their hours before your date day, as they are limited. Admission is free, but donations are always appreciated to support this incredible local gem!

Fourth Stop

Shop & Stroll Through the Village of Webster

After stepping back in time at the museum, take a leisurely stroll down Ridge Road in the Village of Webster, where charming local shops await! Browse unique gifts, home décor, and handcrafted treasures at Lala of Webster and Oh Bella, or pop into Game Craze for a bit of nostalgic fun.

Just a short walk down North Avenue, you'll find The North Bee—a delightful honey and beekeeping shop filled with sweet local finds and all things bee-related.

Whether you're window shopping, picking up a souvenir, or just soaking in the small-town charm, the Village of Webster is the perfect place for a little retail therapy!

Optional Stop

Kittleberger Florist & Gifts

263 North Avenue

Webster, NY 14580

If you're still in the mood to explore and haven't quite had your fill of charming shops, we've got one more stop that's totally worth the (very short) detour.

Just a couple minutes' drive from Main Street—or a longer walk if you're up for it—Kittelberger Florist & Gifts is a local gem that's been serving the Webster community for generations. While it's not technically on the main stretch of the village, it's close enough to feel like part of the experience, and definitely a favorite of ours.

Whether you're just popping in or spending a while soaking it all in, Kittelberger is a lovely way to wrap up your stroll through the Village of Webster before heading off to your final stop.

Finish

Maria's Mexican Restaurant

75 West Main St,
Webster, NY 14580

it's time to indulge in some of the best authentic Mexican food around. Maria's Mexican Restaurant has been a long-time favorite of ours—and of Crystal's family, who've lived here for generations. With the strongest margaritas in town and the most delicious enchiladas, it's a place you won't want to miss.

The Mexican Flag Enchiladas are our personal favorite, and they're always a hit. Pair them with a perfectly mixed margarita and toast to a day filled with wonderful finds, shopping, and good company.

End your adventure in Webster with a meal that celebrates the best of authentic Mexican cuisine in Rochester and the charm of this local gem. We can't think of a better way to close out the day!

Add Your Photos

Keepsakes

Keepsakes

Thank you for joining us on this mystery date adventure! We hope you've enjoyed the delightful experiences and memorable moments we've crafted just for you in Webster, NY.

But the adventure doesn't stop here! Keep exploring exciting mystery dates in other cities and uncover new romantic experiences across the U.S. by visiting our website, DatesInTheStates.com. There, you can purchase both physical copies and digital downloads of our mystery date books. Plus, don't miss out on our Mystery Date Book Club, where you can receive a brand-new mystery date book every month!

Tag us in your date photos on social media! @datesinthestates

About the Creators

Crystal, the writer and creator, is a storyteller at heart. When she's not uncovering hidden gems for the next date night idea, she runs her own digital marketing company, helping small businesses improve their content marketing, increase visibility in their communities, and streamline their online presence.
Visit: crystalstatskey.com

Shane, her husband and partner in adventure, is a dedicated personal trainer and the owner of Beekstar Fitness in Irondequoit, NY. He specializes in working with clients who have limited mobility, helping them build muscle and focus on pain areas so they can regain strength and confidence in their daily lives.
Visit: beekstarfitness.com

Crystal and Shane have explored every U.S. state except Alaska (coming soon!) and are now visiting countries in alphabetical order. Whether road-tripping or curating Mystery Date experiences, they'r always chasing their next adventure.

Local Love

A few local gems in Webster worth exploring on your next date.

SAVERS

WE ALWAYS LOVE A GOOD THRIFT!

980 RIDGE RD, WEBSTER, NY 14580

MAA'S DINER

FUN OLD TIMEY DINER VIBES

2215 EMPIRE BLVD, WEBSTER, NY 14580

ATLANTIC FAMILY RESTAURANT

A BREAKFAST FAVORITE!

888 RIDGE RD, WEBSTER, NY 14580

Want to see your business here? See the next page for details on how to join!

Want to be featured?

MYSTERY DATE BOOK PACKAGES

—

Are you a small business looking to reach new customers? Feature your business in our next Mystery Date Book! Choose from our partnership packages below to connect with couples seeking unique experiences and exclusive deals.

Package One

LOCAL LOVE LISTING

—

A quick shoutout to show you're part of the neighborhood vibe.

Listed in the "Local Love" section of your designated neighborhood date book

Includes business name, address, and social link

Optional: Offer a small promo (e.g., 10% off for book holders)

1 social media shout-out when the book launches

$45

Package Two

FEATURE STOP

—

You're not just a business— you're part of the experience.

Marked as a "Must-Stop" on a Mystery Date

Full-page feature in the book with your story, offerings and photo

Includes 1 social media feature — a dedicated post and story highlighting your business

Note: To ensure each feature is genuine and experience-based, we require a hosted visit prior to inclusion.

$95

Package Three

PARTNER & SELLER

—

Be the spot and the source.

Everything in Tier 2

PLUS: Option to sell the Mystery Date Books at your location

Includes a bulk purchase of 10 books (yours to price + sell)

Keep 100% of the profits from in-store sales

Bonus: Tag as an official pickup location in our promotions

$150

Prices are subject to change

Feel free to reach us at any time by sending us an email to say hi and to learn more! We look forward to hearing from you.

| www.datesinthestates.com | datesinthestatesblog@gmail.com |

Sponsors & Affiliates

Our sponsors and affiliates help make our adventures possible! Explore the amazing brands and businesses that support our community.

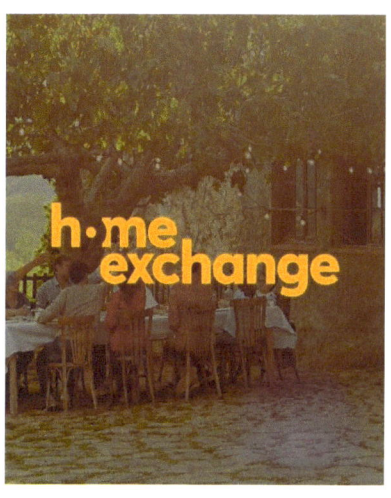

Wanderful

Wanderful is a global community for women who love to travel. Connect, explore, and join a local hub near you!

Join our Book Club!

Join our Mystery Date Book Club and be part of a travel-inspired community, discovering unique local adventures together!

HomeExchange

HomeExchange lets you swap homes with travelers worldwide for authentic, affordable stays. Join today and travel differently!

Shop our books at a store near you!

Little Button Craft	The Pawsitive Cat Cafe	Yesterday's Muse Books	Writers & Books
658 South Ave.	120 East Ave. Ste 100	32 West Main St.	740 University Ave,
Rochester, NY 14620	Rochester, NY 14604	Webster, NY 14580	Rochester, NY 14607
Kittleberger Florist	Flight Wine Bar	Scents by Design	Union Tavern
263 North Avenue,	262 Exchange Blvd,	728 University Ave,	4565 Culver Rd,
Webster, NY 14580	Rochester, NY 14608	Rochester, NY 14607	Irondequoit, NY 14622

DATES IN THE STATES

A COUPLE TRAVELING THE UNITED
STATES ON A BUDGET

Contact Us

🌐

datesinthestates.com

✉

datesinthestatesblog@gmail.com

📍

Based in Rochester, NY

CONNECT WITH US ON SOCIAL!

@DATESINTHESTATES